The Art of Conversion
A Roadmap to Effective Lead Generation

by Mikael da Costa

I would like to start by expressing my deepest gratitude to everyone who has been a part of this incredible journey. First and foremost, I want to thank all the team members at Leadoo for their unwavering support and dedication. Without their hard work, creativity, and passion, this book would not have been possible. To our clients, thank you for entrusting us with your conversion journey and allowing us to be a part of your success stories.

I am also extremely grateful to everyone who has taught and inspired me in the field of digital marketing. Your knowledge, insights, and guidance have been instrumental in shaping my understanding of this dynamic and rapidly evolving industry.

As I share this book with you, I am filled with immense humility and gratitude for the opportunity to pass on the knowledge I have acquired over the years. To you, the reader, thank you for taking the time to explore this book. I truly hope that the insights and strategies shared here will help you unlock the full potential of your website and drive remarkable growth for your business. My sincerest wish is that this book will provide you with valuable knowledge and tools that you can apply to your own digital marketing endeavors.

Once again, thank you all for being a part of this journey, and I hope you enjoy the book.

Mikael da Costa

Introduction
1.1 The Importance of Conversion and Lead Generation

Generating the Right Type of Traffic
2.1 Understanding Your Target Audience
2.2 Advertising Strategies for Attracting Qualified Traffic
2.3 Remarketing: Re-engaging with Your Visitors
2.4 The Power of Content Marketing and SEO

Website Engagement and Visitor Activation
3.1 Designing for User Experience
3.2 Call-to-Action: Turning Visitors into Leads
3.3 Personalization for Enhanced Engagement
3.4 Engaging Website Visitors: Winning Their Trust Through Personalization and Interaction
3.5 Applying the Blue Ocean Strategy to Marketing: Targeting the Right Audiences
3.6 Don't Feed Your Marketing Budget to Your Competitors
3.7 A/B Testing and Optimization

B2B Company Identification and Capturing Buyer Intent
4.1 Identifying and Profiling Your Ideal B2B Customers
4.2 Analyzing Buying Signals and Intent
4.3 Nurturing Leads through the Sales Funnel
4.4 How to use company intent data to drive sales

Interactive Content and Chatbots for Conversions and Lead Generation

5.1 The Rise of Interactive Content
5.2 Types of Interactive Content for Lead Generation
5.3 Implementing Chatbots for Improved Customer Engagement
5.4 Measuring the Impact of Interactive Content and Chatbots
5.5 Reasons to Choose Chatbots over Contact Forms
5.6 Why should you allow your visitors to directly book meetings into your calendar
5.7 Enhancing the customer experience with pricing calculators
5.8 How can discussions help you increase conversions
5.9 How do you make your chatbot stand out from the crowd and produce results?

Analyzing Customer Journeys and Website Analytics
6.1 Mapping the Customer Journey
6.2 Analyzing Website Analytics for Insights
6.3 Identifying Conversion Paths and Drop-off Points
6.4 Leveraging Analytics for Continuous Improvement
6.5 Understanding Attribution Models
6.6 Lead Qualification: Scoring and Prioritizing Leads

Conclusion
7.1 Key Takeaways
7.2 The Future of Conversion and Lead Generation

Introducing Your Author: Mikael da Costa, Serial Entrepreneur and Conversion Expert

My name is Mikael da Costa, and I am an entrepreneur with a genuine interest in digital marketing and conversion optimization. As the founder of Leadoo Marketing Technologies, a pioneering conversion platform, I have made it my mission to assist businesses in activating, converting, and analyzing their website conversions.

With a decade of experience in the digital marketing realm, I've had the opportunity to collaborate with numerous clients, helping them tap into the full potential of their online presence and achieve outstanding results. My hands-on approach and dedication to client success have enabled me to establish enduring partnerships and create a meaningful impact on the businesses I work with.

In 2020, our team's hard work in the industry was acknowledged when Leadoo received the esteemed Marketing Breakthrough Award for the Best Lead Generation Tool for B2B. This recognition not only highlights our team's commitment to innovation and excellence in the field but also demonstrates the value that Leadoo brings to businesses aiming to optimize their website conversions and lead generation strategies.

In this book, I will be sharing the knowledge and tactics that I've gathered throughout my journey, hoping that they will help you unlock your website's full potential and drive significant growth for your business.

Introduction: Turning your website into the best performing sales channel

How many different websites have you visited in the past week? How many online purchases have you made? Often, there's a significant disparity between these two numbers, as we browse through hundreds of websites, consuming their content but not committing to a purchase. Why is it so hard to find what we're looking for?

In today's fiercely competitive business landscape, it has become increasingly essential to not only generate leads but also to shorten the sales cycle and build lasting relationships with customers. The Leadoo philosophy, designed to revolutionize the way businesses approach lead generation and sales, is built upon four key pillars that can propel your organization to new heights.

These pillars are centered around creating a more personal, engaging, and relevant experience for your website visitors. By asking the right questions and understanding your customers' needs and preferences, you can not only generate more leads but also establish trust and credibility with your audience.

By focusing on personalization, value creation, staying informed, and understanding the how and why of customer conversion, the

Leadoo philosophy aims to transform your website into a powerful sales engine. By implementing these strategies and adopting a customer-centric approach, businesses can overcome the challenges of today's digital landscape and turn their website visitors into loyal customers.

So, ask yourself: What can you do to make your website more engaging and relevant to your visitors? How can you better understand and address their needs and preferences? By focusing on these questions and embracing the Leadoo philosophy, you can unlock the full potential of your website and drive impressive growth for your business.

The Leadoo philosophy, designed to revolutionize the way businesses approach lead generation and sales, is built upon four key pillars that can propel your organization to new heights.

Personalize the Customer Experience: At the heart of the Leadoo philosophy is the belief that every customer deserves a hyper-personalized experience tailored to their unique needs and preferences. By understanding your customers and providing them with a customized journey, you can foster stronger connections and drive higher levels of engagement and loyalty.

Create Value and Gather Information: The Leadoo philosophy emphasizes the importance of helping clients validate their needs while simultaneously gathering valuable information that can aid your sales team. By focusing on both creating value and collecting data, you can enhance your understanding of your customers and better serve their needs.

Keep Your Sales Team Informed: Empower your sales team with up-to-date information about your customers, enabling them to engage with prospects more effectively and close deals faster. By keeping your sales team informed, you can ensure that they have the insights and tools needed to excel in their roles and drive success for your organization.

Understand Why and How: The Leadoo philosophy encourages organizations to measure the entire customer journey and gain a comprehensive understanding of why and how clients convert. By analyzing and learning from this data, you can optimize your marketing and sales efforts, leading to increased conversion rates and a stronger bottom line.

In this book, we will delve deep into the Leadoo philosophy, offering insights, strategies, and techniques that can transform your approach to lead generation and sales. By adopting these principles and implementing the lessons learned, you will be well on your way to creating a more effective, efficient, and customer-centric organization that excels in the modern business world.

1.1 The Importance of Conversion and Lead Generation

In today's digital landscape, businesses face a myriad of challenges. Competition is not only growing but also becoming increasingly global, making it essential for companies to stand out in their local markets and beyond. With more information available than ever before, consumers are taking control of their purchasing journey, often resulting in longer sales cycles.

As a business owner or marketer, it's crucial to understand that activating website visitors is more challenging than ever before. Attention spans are shrinking, making it vital to capture and maintain your audience's interest as quickly as possible. People now expect personalized content that caters to their needs and preferences, further emphasizing the importance of delivering an exceptional user experience.

In this era, user experience reigns supreme, even surpassing the long-held belief that content is king. As such, businesses must prioritize conversion and lead generation strategies that focus on creating a seamless, engaging, and personalized experience for every website visitor. Embracing emerging technologies, such as chatbots, interactive content, and website personalization, can play a crucial role in enhancing user experience and driving conversions.

Chatbots, for instance, have revolutionized customer engagement by offering real-time, personalized assistance that streamlines the user's journey on your website. Interactive content, such as quizzes, calculators, and polls, adds an engaging and dynamic element to your site, encouraging visitors to interact and share their information. Website personalization tailors the browsing experience to each visitor, making them feel valued and understood, which increases the likelihood of conversion.

To stay ahead in this ever-evolving landscape, it's essential to master the art of conversion and lead generation, incorporating cutting-edge technologies and techniques to create a memorable and effective user experience. In the following sections, I'll be sharing proven strategies and insights to help you optimize your website, engage your visitors effectively, and ultimately drive business growth through increased conversions and leads.

Generating the Right Type of Traffic

2.1 Understanding Your Target Audience: Focusing on Qualified Traffic

Many companies tend to concentrate on the number of page views or visitors their website receives, which can often be a misleading metric for success. Instead, businesses should shift their focus to measuring the amount of qualified traffic, as this provides a better understanding of how well their website attracts the right audience.

Qualified traffic refers to website visitors who have a higher likelihood of converting due to their alignment with your ideal customer profile. To better understand what type of traffic is qualified, you should consider the following aspects:

- Ask your website visitors questions: By asking relevant questions, you can gather information about your visitors and determine whether they are part of your target audience. For example, if you are a company selling pre-built houses, you could ask visitors whether they already own a plot of land. This would help you filter out those who are not yet ready to purchase a pre-built house, as they do not meet a key requirement.

- Identify the industries of your B2B visitors: In the B2B sector, it is essential to recognize which companies visit your website and whether they belong to your target industry. By analyzing the industries of your visitors, you can focus your marketing efforts on attracting more qualified leads from the desired sectors.

One common issue that many businesses face is a low website conversion rate, with industry averages often falling below 2%. This can be attributed to a variety of factors, including a lack of focus on attracting the right audience. When companies prioritize cost-effective channels to acquire traffic, they may inadvertently attract a higher number of unqualified visitors. Without analyzing the ideal customer profiles and refining their marketing strategies accordingly, businesses might be growing the number of wrong type of visitors, resulting in lower conversion rates.

As a marketer, it is crucial to define what qualified traffic means for your business and measure the numbers of qualified visitors coming to your website. This approach allows you to make informed decisions and optimize your marketing strategies for better results. By focusing on attracting qualified traffic, you can increase your website conversion rates and achieve greater success.

To gain a deeper understanding of your target audience and their preferences, it's essential to collect and analyze data from various sources, such as website analytics, customer feedback, and market research. This data-driven approach will enable you to tailor your marketing efforts to better resonate with your ideal customer profiles.

One tool that can help you with this task is Leadoo Website Analytics. This easy-to-use tool has built-in filters that make it simple to analyze your website performance across different ideal customer profile segments. By utilizing such tools, you can gain valuable insights into your target audience and tailor your marketing efforts accordingly, ultimately increasing the effectiveness of your conversion and lead generation strategies.

2.2 Advertising Strategies for Attracting Qualified Traffic

Attracting qualified traffic to your website is crucial for increasing conversion rates and driving business growth. However, in the modern digital landscape, buyer journeys have become longer and more complex, involving multiple touchpoints across various channels. This complexity makes it challenging to measure the effectiveness of advertising efforts and determine which channels are best suited for different stages of the customer journey.

In this chapter, we will explore various advertising strategies and tactics to help you attract qualified traffic, with a focus on targeting the right audience, understanding the role of different channels, and leveraging data to optimize your efforts.

- **The Role of Different Channels in the Customer Journey:** Different advertising channels often serve different purposes in the customer journey. For example, Facebook is typically the cheapest channel and can be effective in attracting users at the top of the marketing funnel who may not have been aware of your brand before. Facebook can be a great platform for promoting webinars, whitepapers, or other top-of-the-funnel content. On the other hand, Google Ads, particularly search ads, target users who are actively searching for specific products or services, making them more likely to be in the consideration or decision stage of the customer journey. Understanding the strengths and weaknesses of each channel will help you develop a well-rounded advertising strategy that effectively targets your ideal audience throughout their journey.

- **Lookalike Audiences:** In some cases, it can be challenging to directly target your ideal audience using traditional advertising methods. For example, there is no direct targeting option for plot owners in the pre-built house market. However, by asking your website visitors relevant questions and capturing their responses, you can create lookalike audiences based on the characteristics of your most qualified visitors. Lookalike audiences are groups of users who share similar attributes, behaviors, or interests with your ideal customers. By targeting these lookalike audiences, you can expand your reach and attract more qualified traffic to your website.

- **B2B Targeting Strategies:** B2B advertising often requires a more targeted approach to reach specific companies or industries with unique needs. For example, a logistics company may offer a variety of services, but a large portion of their leads may only be interested in one-time transportation. By asking website visitors whether they need one-time or regular transportation services, the company can qualify leads and create lookalike or remarketing audiences based on the most highly qualified visitors. This approach allows them to focus their advertising efforts on attracting the right audience and generating higher-quality leads.

In addition to these strategies, consider the following tips and tactics to enhance your advertising efforts and attract more qualified traffic:

- Utilize Retargeting and Remarketing: Retargeting and remarketing campaigns allow you to re-engage with users who have previously interacted with your brand, either by visiting your website or engaging with your content on social media platforms. These campaigns are particularly effective for nurturing prospects and driving conversions, as they enable you to deliver personalized content and offers based on the user's previous interactions with your brand.

- Test and Optimize Ad Creatives: Continuously test and optimize your ad creatives to ensure they resonate with your target audience and effectively convey your message. This process involves experimenting with different headlines, images, and calls to action, as well as analyzing performance data to identify what works best for your audience.

- Leverage Data-Driven Targeting: Use data from your website analytics, CRM, and other sources to inform your targeting decisions and refine your advertising strategy. This approach allows you to identify patterns and trends in user behavior, preferences, and demographics, helping you create more relevant and effective advertising campaigns.

By implementing these advertising strategies and tactics, you can better target your ideal audience, effectively engage with them at different stages of the customer journey, and ultimately drive more qualified traffic to your website. By focusing on attracting the right audience, you can increase your chances of driving higher conversion rates and achieving greater success in your marketing efforts.

2.3 Remarketing: Re-engaging with Your Visitors

Remarketing is a powerful digital marketing strategy that allows businesses to re-engage with users who have previously interacted with their website or content. By leveraging remarketing techniques, companies can reinforce their brand message, create tailored offers, and improve the likelihood of converting prospects into customers. In this chapter, we will discuss the importance of remarketing, particularly in the context of the logistics and pre-made house industries, and explore how different advertising platforms like Facebook and LinkedIn can be leveraged for remarketing purposes.

Remarketing is essential because it helps businesses remain top of mind for potential customers who may have visited their website but did not convert. It is especially important in industries where the buying process is more complex and involves longer decision-making cycles, such as logistics and pre-made house sectors. By staying in touch with prospects through remarketing, businesses can nurture relationships and maintain a consistent brand presence, increasing the likelihood of conversion over time.

Using the logistics and pre-made house examples with a focus on interactive content:

- Logistics: Through the use of interactive content, a logistics company can gather valuable information about their website visitors, such as whether they require one-time or regular transportation services. By identifying high-value leads (those needing regular transportation), the company can then focus most of their remarketing budget on targeting these prospects. This targeted approach ensures that their advertising dollars are spent on the most valuable audience segment, increasing the chances of conversion and ultimately generating a better return on investment.

- Pre-made houses: In the pre-made house industry, interactive content can help companies determine which website visitors already have a plot and are therefore more likely to build a house soon. Armed with this information, the company can focus its remarketing efforts on these "ready-to-build" prospects, rather than those who are simply daydreaming about building a house someday. By concentrating their advertising budget on targeting the right audience segment, the company increases the likelihood of converting qualified leads and driving sales.

Facebook and LinkedIn are two popular platforms for remarketing, each with its own set of advantages and challenges. Facebook is typically a more cost-effective platform, but it can be harder to target specific audiences unless you capture data from your website using interactive content. By collecting valuable information about your website visitors through interactive content, you can create highly targeted remarketing audiences on Facebook, ensuring that your ads reach the most relevant prospects. On the other hand, LinkedIn offers more precise targeting options for B2B industries but comes at a higher cost. By leveraging the insights gained from interactive content, you can make the most of your remarketing budget on both platforms, optimizing your campaigns for maximum impact and efficiency.

When setting up your first remarketing campaigns, there are several important factors to consider in order to maximize the effectiveness of your efforts. Here are some key aspects to keep in mind:

1. Define your goals: Before launching your remarketing campaign, it is crucial to have a clear understanding of your objectives. Are you looking to increase brand awareness, drive website traffic, generate leads, or boost sales? Having a

well-defined goal will help you create more targeted ads and measure the success of your campaign.

2. Segment your audience: Not all website visitors are equal, so it's essential to segment your audience based on their behavior, interests, or demographic characteristics. By creating separate remarketing lists for different audience segments, you can tailor your ads to resonate with each group and improve the relevance of your messaging.

3. Choose the right platforms: Select the advertising platforms that are best suited for your target audience and objectives. For example, Facebook and Instagram might be more appropriate for B2C campaigns, while LinkedIn is better suited for B2B audiences. Also, consider using multiple platforms to reach your audience across various channels and touchpoints.

4. Create compelling ad creatives: Your remarketing ads should be visually appealing, with clear messaging and a strong call to action. Make sure to test different ad formats, such as image, video, or carousel ads, to see which resonates best with your audience.

5. Set the right frequency cap and ad scheduling: To avoid overwhelming your audience with ads, set a frequency cap that limits the number of times a user sees your ad within a specific time frame. Additionally, use ad scheduling to run your ads during the most relevant times of the day or week for your target audience.

6.   Monitor and optimize: Regularly analyze your campaign performance and make adjustments as needed. Keep an eye on key performance indicators (KPIs) such as click-through rates, conversion rates, and cost per conversion. Continuously test different ad creatives, targeting options, and bidding strategies to optimize your campaigns for better results.

7.   Evaluate campaign success with attribution modeling: To gain a comprehensive understanding of your remarketing campaigns' effectiveness, use attribution modeling techniques. Attribution modeling helps you determine the value of each touchpoint in the customer journey, allowing you to make more informed decisions about your marketing efforts. Leadoo Source Analytics is a fully set up attribution modeling tool that simplifies the process of tracking and analyzing your marketing channels' performance. By leveraging Leadoo Source Analytics, you can easily assess the contribution of each marketing channel and optimize your marketing strategies for better results and improved ROI. This valuable insight will guide your future decisions on budget allocation, campaign strategies, and overall marketing efforts.

By taking these factors into account when setting up your first remarketing campaigns, you will be better prepared to engage your audience, drive conversions, and achieve your marketing goals.

2.4 The Power of Content Marketing and SEO

Content marketing and Search Engine Optimization (SEO) are two essential components of a successful digital marketing strategy. While they are often discussed in terms of driving traffic to a website, their true potential lies in their ability to move prospects further down the sales funnel and generate qualified leads. In this chapter, we will discuss the importance of content marketing and SEO, the challenges of passive content, and the opportunities presented by interactive content to maximize your marketing efforts.

1.   Content Marketing and SEO: An Overview
Content marketing involves creating valuable, relevant, and engaging content that attracts and retains your target audience. It helps build trust, credibility, and brand authority, ultimately leading to increased conversions. SEO, on the other hand, is the process of optimizing your website and content to rank higher in search engine results, making it more visible to users searching for information related to your industry or products.
Both content marketing and SEO work together to improve your online presence, increase website traffic, and generate leads. Research has shown that companies with a strong content marketing strategy have conversion rates that are nearly six times higher than their competitors without one. Furthermore, 61% of marketers say improving SEO and growing their organic presence is their top inbound marketing priority.

2.   The Limitations of Passive Content

Many businesses focus solely on creating blogs and landing pages to attract visitors to their website. While this approach can be effective in driving traffic, it often falls short in terms of lead generation and conversion. Passive content lacks the interactivity and personalization needed to engage users and move them further down the sales funnel.

3. Harnessing the Power of Interactive Content

Interactive content has the potential to transform your content marketing and SEO efforts by engaging users and converting them into qualified leads. By offering dynamic content such as quizzes, calculators, or interactive infographics, you can provide users with a personalized and engaging experience that encourages them to take action. When combined with a strong SEO strategy, interactive content can drive more targeted traffic to your website, increasing the likelihood of conversion and maximizing the return on your SEO investment.

4. Turning SEO Investment into Qualified Leads

By incorporating interactive content into your content marketing and SEO strategy, you can turn your website traffic into qualified leads. This can be achieved by asking your visitors questions related to their interests, needs, or challenges and then providing them with personalized recommendations or solutions. For example, a company selling pre-made houses could use an interactive quiz to determine a user's budget, design preferences, and plot availability. This information can then be used to offer tailored suggestions, capture user information, and ultimately generate more qualified leads.

In conclusion, the power of content marketing and SEO extends beyond merely increasing website traffic. By incorporating interactive content into your strategy, you can better engage your audience, move them further down the sales funnel, and turn your SEO investment into qualified leads. This approach not only improves your conversion rates but also maximizes the overall effectiveness of your digital marketing efforts.

Website Engagement and Visitor Activation

3.1 Designing for User Experience: Catering to Different Stages of the Buyer's Journey

A well-designed user experience (UX) is essential for guiding prospects through the various stages of the buyer's journey. Each stage requires a different approach to ensure that your website effectively serves your customers' needs and drives them toward conversion. In this chapter, we will discuss the importance of designing your website to cater to the different stages of the buyer's journey, and how to tailor your content and UX to achieve this.

- Awareness Stage: Building Understanding and Trust

During the awareness stage, your primary goal as a marketer is to show that you understand your prospects' problems and provide them with valuable information and resources. To achieve this, design your website with informative and engaging content such as blog posts, whitepapers, or educational videos. Make it easy for visitors to find this content through clear navigation and effective on-page SEO.

- Interested Stage: Educating and Guiding

When prospects reach the interested stage, they have acknowledged their problem and are actively seeking a solution. Your job is to prove the need for your product or service and educate them on how to make a purchase decision. Utilize case studies, testimonials, and comparison charts to showcase the benefits of your offering. Design your website to include clear calls-to-action (CTAs) that guide them to relevant resources or sales pages.

- **Consideration Stage: Demonstrating Your Value**

At the consideration stage, prospects are evaluating their options and looking for the best fit. Your goal is to prove that your product or service is the optimal choice. Design your website with personalized content and experiences tailored to your target audience. Leverage tools such as live chat, chatbots, or interactive content to answer questions, address concerns, and showcase your unique selling points.

- **Decision Stage: Streamlining the Path to Conversion**

Finally, during the decision stage, your main objective is to make it as easy as possible for prospects to convert. Optimize your website for user experience by reducing friction in the conversion process. This may involve simplifying your contact forms, offering multiple contact options, or providing clear pricing and purchase information. Additionally, ensure that your sales team is equipped to respond promptly to inquiries, helping prospects move smoothly through the final stage of the journey.

By designing your website to cater to the various stages of the buyer's journey, you acknowledge the fact that different visitors require different information based on their current stage. A one-size-fits-all approach often fails to serve anyone effectively. This is where interactive content becomes a powerful tool, allowing each visitor to explore their journey on their own terms and receive the personalized information they need.

People's behavior has changed over time, and they are now tuning out traditional marketing tactics. To attract customers, marketers need to provide them with engaging, valuable, and interactive content that they can connect with. It is essential to adapt to this need for on-demand, self-guided experiences.

Studies show that 70% of the buyer journey is completed before sales is even contacted, which means customers are in full control and prefer to serve themselves whenever it is convenient for them. By incorporating interactive content, you can cater to this preference, acting on-demand to guide, educate, and entertain your customers even when you're not directly involved.

Embracing this tailored approach, with interactive content at its core, will not only help you better serve your customers but also increase the likelihood of conversion, maximizing the success of your digital marketing efforts.

3.2 Call-to-Action: Turning Visitors into Leads with Interactive Content

With visitors at different stages of their buyer's journey, it's essential to have call-to-action (CTA) elements that appeal to everyone. Interactive content plays a crucial role in engaging your audience and converting visitors into leads.

One might wonder why interactive content is so effective. The answer lies in its ability to create a conversation with your audience, bringing the dynamism and persuasive power of in-person interactions to various digital platforms. Interactive content works well because humans have a natural inclination to engage in activities that involve self-assessment, competition, comparison, and sharing opinions. Moreover, interactive content provides a personalized experience for users based on their responses, which makes it highly appealing to them.

In terms of delivering value, interactive content benefits both prospects and marketers. Customers seek valuable content that addresses their pain points, answers questions, or provides essential information. Interactive content excels in delivering personalized results in real time, guiding prospects toward solutions tailored to their specific challenges.

By participating in interactive content, users not only receive the information they need but also generate valuable insights for marketers. As prospects engage with interactive content, they provide detailed profile information about their pain points, challenges, goals, and thought processes. This data can help with lead scoring, persona identification, prospect qualification, and guiding the audience through their buyer's journey.

As a marketer, you can utilize this information to follow up with targeted content that addresses your audience's needs and helps solve their problems. Interactive content essentially acts as a virtual sales development representative, asking and answering questions on your behalf.

We will delve into various strategies for incorporating interactive content into your CTAs. This encompasses tailoring CTAs to different stages of the buyer's journey, designing engaging and persuasive interactive content, utilizing interactive content for lead capture and nurturing, optimizing CTAs for maximum conversions, and measuring the success of your interactive content and CTAs.

Interactive content serves as a powerful tool to educate, entertain, and engage your audience. It demands the participants' active engagement beyond just reading or watching, and in return, they receive real-time, hyper-relevant results they genuinely care about.

By harnessing the power of interactive content in your CTAs, you can effectively convert more visitors into leads, ultimately optimizing the success of your digital marketing efforts.

3.3 Personalization for Enhanced Engagement

In today's digital landscape, personalization has become a critical factor in engaging and retaining users. As consumers become increasingly discerning, they expect experiences that cater specifically to their needs and preferences. Personalization has become a powerful force in the world of marketing and customer experience. It not only helps create a more engaging and relevant experience for users but also drives better conversion rates and customer loyalty. As consumer behavior continues to evolve, businesses must adapt and focus on providing personalized experiences to stay competitive.

Interactive content plays a crucial role in personalizing user experiences. By allowing users to actively engage with content that is tailored to their specific needs and preferences, businesses can create a more meaningful connection with their audience. This, in turn, increases the likelihood of conversions and fosters long-term customer loyalty. Website personalization tools like Sitecore, Frosmo, Mutinity, or Hubspot can significantly improve your personalization efforts. These tools enable you to customize various aspects of your website based on user behavior, preferences, and other factors. However, personalizing an entire page can be challenging and time-consuming.

This is where Leadoo, a powerful interactive content platform, comes into play. Leadoo allows you to easily personalize interactive content based on various factors, including revenue, industry, headcount, page visits, X page, previous discussion data, CRM data, existing or new clients, sales reps, client stage, and previous conversions. By harnessing Leadoo's capabilities, you can create targeted, engaging content that appeals to your audience and drives conversions.

As mentioned earlier, today's consumers expect personalized experiences. They have grown accustomed to platforms like Spotify and Netflix, which provide tailored recommendations based on their preferences and behavior. As a result, they now expect similar levels of personalization from other businesses and services. Personalization is no longer a novelty but a necessity. Businesses that fail to adapt and provide tailored experiences risk losing customers to competitors who can cater to their needs more effectively.

While personalization is essential, it's crucial to strike a balance between providing tailored experiences and respecting user privacy. Overly intrusive personalization can make users feel uncomfortable and lead to a negative perception of your brand. To avoid this, ensure that your personalization efforts are transparent, and give users control over the data you collect and how you use it.

By leveraging the power of interactive content, website personalization tools, and platforms like Leadoo, you can create engaging, personalized experiences that resonate with your audience. These tailored experiences not only improve user satisfaction but also drive higher conversion rates and overall success for your digital marketing efforts. As the world continues to evolve, personalization will become even more critical for businesses looking to stand out and thrive in an increasingly competitive landscape.

3.4 Engaging Website Visitors: Winning Their Trust Through Personalization and Interaction

Five years ago, I moved to the suburbs with my 2.5-year-old daughter. Soon after, we noticed a squirrel visiting our backyard every day, which greatly excited my daughter. Wanting to make the most of this opportunity, I bought nuts and tried to feed the squirrel.

Despite having what the squirrel wanted, it would run away every time we approached. It took two weeks for the squirrel to finally pick up nuts from my hand, as long as my daughter was inside. The question is, why did it take so long? And what does this have to do with marketing?

Capture Their Attention
Just like the squirrel, website visitors need to be convinced that you have something valuable for them. With an average attention span of 6-8 seconds, you need to grab their attention quickly.

As traditional media companies struggle, the Huffington Post has been growing. Ariana Huffington once said that traditional media companies haven't realized there are no passive readers anymore. This raises the question: Are there passive website visitors anymore? What kind of interactions could you develop on your website that would grab users' attention and engage them?

Personalize the Journey & Win Their Trust
Even though I had what the squirrel wanted, it didn't eat from my hand immediately. I needed to prove my intentions were genuine. The same applies to marketing.

You need to understand what your website visitors want and what questions they have in mind. Personalize the content based on their buying stage, tailoring the information to their needs at each stage.

Take solar panels as an example. A visitor searching for general information about the benefits of solar panels and someone who knows they are interested and is looking for the best product require different content.

Analyze the Results
Lastly, analyze the results of all your experiments, because with lead generation, one word can make or break the outcome.

For instance, we had a customer selling Yale Doorman locks who had many visitors but no conversions. We built an interactive in-page bot, and two weeks later, we saw increased time on the page and many interactions. Still, there were no leads.

The key takeaway is that engaging and winning the trust of website visitors is crucial. Just like the squirrel needed time and personalized attention to trust me, visitors need personalized, interactive content to feel engaged and trust your intentions. By capturing their attention, personalizing the journey, and analyzing the results, you can create lasting relationships with your website visitors and ultimately convert them into leads.

3.5 Applying the Blue Ocean Strategy to Marketing: Targeting the Right Audiences

The Blue Ocean Strategy, one of the most influential marketing books ever written, teaches us a valuable lesson about targeting the right audience. This principle aligns perfectly with successful marketing strategies in today's competitive landscape.

The Blue Ocean Strategy Theory
According to the theory, the market is divided into two categories: active buyers and passive buyers.

Active buyers consist of:

- 3% who are currently purchasing the product you offer
- 6% who plan to purchase the product within the next 90 days

Passive buyers include:

- 30% who are not thinking about the product you offer
- 30% who are not interested
- 30% who are definitely not interested

Companies often struggle with inbound marketing due to the limitations of reaching their target audience. Google AdWords tends to target active buyers who are already purchasing, while content marketing distributed through LinkedIn, Facebook, Google Display, or email marketing mostly attracts passive buyers.

The challenge with passive buyers is the need to activate them, and contact forms typically don't achieve that goal.

Bridging the Gap: From Passive to Active Buyers
Content marketing generates traffic, but contact forms often fail to convert that traffic into leads or customers. To resolve this issue, businesses must adopt innovative strategies to engage and activate passive buyers.

1.   Personalization: Tailor your content and marketing messages to address the specific needs and interests of your audience. This approach will make your content more relevant and engaging, increasing the likelihood of conversion.

2.   Interactivity: Encourage website visitors to engage with your content through interactive elements such as quizzes, polls,

or live chats. These tools can help you better understand your audience and guide them towards becoming active buyers.

3. Value-driven approach: Offer valuable resources and incentives to entice passive buyers to take action. This could include free trials, exclusive discounts, or educational content that addresses their pain points.

4. Nurture campaigns: Develop targeted email marketing campaigns to nurture passive buyers and maintain their interest in your product or service. Regular touchpoints can help to establish trust and keep your brand top of mind.

By incorporating these strategies into your marketing efforts, you can effectively target the right audiences and tap into the vast potential of passive buyers. By doing so, you'll create a blue ocean of opportunity for your business, setting it apart from competitors and driving growth.

3.6 Don't Feed Your Marketing Budget to Your Competitors

If the buyer isn't sure they're making the right decision, they won't buy. Instead, they'll turn to your competition for support if you aren't able to provide it. As we discussed in previous chapters, you have people across different stages of the buyer journey, and you need to be able to cater to their personal needs.

A story that really brought this to life happened a year ago when my wife saw a Kärcher ad about window washing machines. It was springtime, and our windows needed to be cleaned, so the timing was perfect. They had created a great ad, targeting the right audience at the right time.

My wife had never thought about window washing machines in the past, so before buying, she had to do a bit of research. However, the only difference she saw between the products was the price. The ad she had seen was from a company called "Taloon.com." As she couldn't understand any other major differences between the products, she turned to me for advice. Well, as you can imagine, I'm not an enthusiastic window cleaner myself, so I didn't see any significant differences either. If I had to choose, I would have picked the cheapest one, but only if it could do the job we needed. In this sense, pricing was important to us; we didn't want to spend more than necessary, but we also didn't want to buy a product that didn't fit our needs.

In this case, Taloon.com had done a great job making my wife aware of a problem and getting her interested. However, since she needed help choosing the right product or validating her decision, she didn't get the support she needed from Taloon.com. I told her to go to the nearest hardware store, K-Rauta, where she received the assistance she needed. She went there and bought the window washing machine from them. This is a great example of a company that created excellent advertising but, due to a lack of support on their website, fed their marketing budget to their competitor.

Imagine if Taloon.com had created an interactive quiz, "Let me help you find the right product for you." It could have asked questions like how many windows you have, whether they are one or two-piece windows, and if they are big or small. Based on your answers, the quiz could have provided the right product recommendation for you. By offering personalized support to potential customers, businesses can avoid losing sales to competitors and make the most of their marketing budgets.

3.7 A/B Testing and Optimization

In the ever-evolving digital landscape, businesses must continuously adapt and optimize their marketing strategies to stay competitive and achieve desired results. A/B testing and optimization are essential components of any successful digital marketing strategy, allowing marketers to make data-driven decisions and improve the overall user experience.

A/B testing, also known as split testing, is a process where two or more versions of a web page, email, ad, or other marketing assets are compared against each other to determine which performs better. By showing different variations to users and tracking their engagement, marketers can gain valuable insights into what resonates best with their audience. These insights can then be used to make informed decisions about content, design, and overall strategy.

The primary goal of A/B testing is to optimize conversion rates, whether it's generating leads, driving sales, or increasing user engagement. By testing different variations, marketers can identify which elements are most effective at driving desired actions and refine their strategies accordingly. The process of A/B testing and optimization typically involves the following steps:

1. Identify a goal: Clearly define the objective of your test, such as increasing sign-ups, improving click-through rates, or boosting sales. This goal will help guide your testing process and ensure you're focusing on the most relevant metrics.

2. Develop a hypothesis: Based on your goal, develop a hypothesis about which changes to your marketing asset might lead to better performance. This hypothesis should be based on data, user feedback, or industry best practices.

3. Create variations: Develop multiple versions of your marketing asset, each incorporating the changes outlined in your hypothesis. For instance, you might test different headlines, calls-to-action, or design elements.

4. Split your audience: Randomly assign users to see one of the variations, ensuring that each group is statistically similar in terms of demographics, behavior, and other relevant factors.

5.   Collect and analyze data: Track user engagement with each variation and compare the results to determine which version performed better. Use statistical analysis to ensure the differences in performance are significant and not due to chance.

6.   Implement the winning variation: If the test results show a clear winner, implement the winning variation on your website, email, or ad. This will help you achieve your goal more effectively and maximize the return on your marketing investment.

7.   Iterate and optimize: Continue testing and optimizing your marketing assets to identify further improvements and adapt to changing user preferences and industry trends.

A/B testing and optimization can be applied to various aspects of digital marketing, including website design, email marketing, social media advertising, and search engine optimization. For instance, interactive content can also benefit from A/B testing, allowing you to identify which types of content and engagement techniques are most effective at driving conversions.

Platforms like Leadoo make it easy to set up and manage A/B tests, allowing marketers to focus on refining their strategies and driving better results. By embracing A/B testing and optimization, businesses can continuously improve their marketing efforts, creating more engaging and personalized experiences for their audience and maximizing their digital marketing success.

41

B2B Company Identification and Capturing Buyer Intent

4.1 Identifying and Profiling Your Ideal B2B Customers

A key aspect of any successful B2B marketing strategy is identifying and profiling your ideal customers. Understanding who your target audience is and what drives their decision-making process enables you to create more effective marketing campaigns and tailor your messaging to resonate with them. In this chapter, we will discuss the concept of reverse IP tracking and how it can help you better understand and profile your ideal B2B customers.

Reverse IP Tracking: What Is It and How Does It Work?

Reverse IP tracking is a technology that allows businesses to identify the companies visiting their website by analyzing their IP addresses. When a user visits your website, their IP address is logged, and reverse IP tracking tools can match this address to a specific company. This provides valuable insights into which companies are engaging with your content, allowing you to better understand your audience and tailor your marketing efforts accordingly.

How Reverse IP Tracking Can Help You Reach the Right Customers

1. Identifying potential leads: By tracking the companies visiting your website, you can identify new business opportunities and focus your sales efforts on those that are already engaged with your brand.

2. Understanding visitor behavior: Reverse IP tracking allows you to analyze the behavior of your website visitors, such as which pages they visit, how long they spend on each page, and the actions they take. This information can help you identify which aspects of your website and content are most appealing to your target audience, enabling you to optimize your marketing strategy.

3. Personalizing your marketing efforts: With insights into the companies visiting your website, you can create more targeted and personalized marketing campaigns. For example, you can segment your email marketing list based on industry or company size to send more relevant content to each group.

4. Measuring the effectiveness of your marketing efforts: By tracking the companies visiting your website, you can determine if your marketing efforts are successfully attracting the right audience. If you notice a high number of visitors from industries or companies that are not part of your target market, you may need to adjust your marketing strategy to better reach your ideal customers.

5. Enhancing lead qualification: Knowing which companies are visiting your website can help you prioritize and qualify leads

more effectively. By focusing on companies that have demonstrated interest in your content, your sales team can be more efficient and close deals faster.

In conclusion, reverse IP tracking is a valuable tool for B2B marketers looking to better understand and profile their ideal customers. By identifying the companies visiting your website and analyzing their behavior, you can create more targeted and effective marketing campaigns that resonate with your audience. Moreover, tools like Leadoo can help you easily implement reverse IP tracking and gain valuable insights to optimize your marketing efforts and drive better results.

4.2 Analyzing Buying Signals and Intent

Understanding buying signals and customer intent is crucial in today's competitive B2B landscape for businesses to stay ahead of the competition and close deals faster. With interactive content and reverse IP data, you can gather valuable insights about your potential customers, enabling you to analyze their buying signals and intent more effectively. Interactive content enables you to engage your website visitors in a conversation, gathering valuable information about their interests and preferences. By using reverse IP tracking, you can identify the companies visiting your website and better understand if you are reaching the right customers. Combining the insights from interactive content and reverse IP data allows you to paint a clearer picture of your potential customers' buying signals and intent.

Once you have collected and analyzed the data from interactive content and reverse IP tracking, it's essential to make the most of this information by connecting it to your CRM and marketing automation tools. By integrating this data into your CRM, sales representatives can access real-time information about what clients are interested in, helping them tailor their approach and close deals more effectively. Furthermore, using the insights from interactive content and reverse IP data, you can create personalized marketing automation campaigns based on the specific interests and preferences of your potential customers. This targeted approach ensures that your marketing efforts resonate with your audience, driving higher engagement and conversion rates.

For example, consider a logistics company that uses interactive content to gather information about their potential customers' transportation needs. They could ask questions about the type of transportation required, frequency, and other specific requirements. By combining this data with reverse IP tracking, they can identify the company behind the inquiry, even if the visitor did not provide contact information. This information can be integrated into their CRM, enabling sales representatives to better understand the potential customer's needs and tailor their approach accordingly.

Another example could be a golf company that offers corporate event packages. They could create a pricing calculator that asks visitors about the type of event they want to host, the number of attendees, the desired date, and any additional services they might be interested in. Even if the visitor leaves the calculator without providing their contact details, the golf company could still connect the answers to the corresponding company using reverse IP technology. This information can then be used to personalize marketing automation campaigns and help sales representatives better understand the potential customer's needs.

In conclusion, analyzing buying signals and intent using interactive content and reverse IP data can provide valuable insights into your potential customers, allowing you to tailor your marketing and sales strategies more effectively. By integrating this data with your CRM and marketing automation tools, you can enhance your overall marketing efforts and improve your chances of closing deals with the right customers.

4.3 Nurturing Leads through the Sales Funnel

Nurturing leads through the sales funnel is an essential process for any business that wants to effectively convert prospects into paying customers. With the wealth of data available in CRM and marketing automation systems, it's crucial to leverage this information to provide personalized experiences on your website.

Traditional websites often rely heavily on "contact us" forms as the primary method of engagement with potential customers. However, this approach can be limiting, especially for visitors who are already customers or are in the sales cycle. Instead, businesses should be using interactive content to personalize experiences based on CRM data and the individual's stage in the sales funnel.

By utilizing interactive content, you can create a more engaging and customized experience for each visitor. This not only helps in building a stronger relationship with your prospects but also increases the chances of converting them into customers. As a prospect moves through the sales funnel, their needs and interests change. By personalizing the content and interactions based on their stage in the funnel, you can provide the right information and support at the right time.

For example, if a visitor is in the early stages of the sales funnel, they might be more interested in educational content that helps them understand the value and benefits of your products or services. Interactive content such as quizzes, calculators, or assessments can be used to engage and educate these prospects, helping them progress to the next stage in the funnel.

On the other hand, visitors who are further along in the sales process may already be familiar with your offerings and are now considering whether to make a purchase. In this case, personalized interactive content that highlights case studies, testimonials, or product comparisons can be more effective in addressing their concerns and nudging them towards making a decision.

By leveraging CRM data, you can also create more targeted and relevant experiences for your existing customers. For instance, you can use this information to upsell or cross-sell related products and services, provide personalized support, or offer loyalty incentives to strengthen the customer relationship.

Nurturing leads through the sales funnel requires a tailored approach that takes into account each prospect's stage in the process and the information available in your CRM and marketing automation systems. By using interactive content to create personalized experiences based on this data, you can guide your prospects more effectively through the sales funnel, ultimately increasing your chances of converting them into loyal customers.

4.4 How to use company intent data to drive sales

Leveraging company intent data can significantly enhance your marketing and sales efforts by providing valuable insights into the behavior and interests of your prospects. By identifying and acting on these insights, you can improve lead conversion and better prioritize your sales pipeline.

1. Use Cases for Company Intent Data
a. Alerting Salespeople of Prospects Visiting Your Website: Enable your sales team to take timely action by notifying them when prospects from their pipeline visit your website. This real-time information allows salespeople to engage with the prospects when they are most interested and increase the chances of conversion.

b. Re-engaging Frozen or Lost Deals: Reactivate stalled or lost deals by tracking when these prospects revisit your website. This re-engagement can reignite interest in your products or services and present new opportunities for conversion.

2. Benefits of Using Sales Alerts
Sales alerts can provide valuable real-time information to your sales team, enabling them to act more effectively and efficiently. Some of the key benefits include:

a. Timely and Relevant Engagement: Sales alerts notify salespeople about the website visits, actions, and buying signals of prospects in their pipeline, allowing them to engage with these prospects in a personalized and timely manner.

b. Calendar Integration: Sales alerts can be integrated with your team's calendar, making it easy for prospects to schedule meetings and further engage with your sales team.

3. Automating Sales Alerts and Focusing on Results

Sales alert tools offer extensive automation capabilities, enabling you to create specific rules for sending alerts based on the prospect's behavior and stage in the sales pipeline. By tailoring these rules, you can ensure that your sales team focuses on the areas where they excel and where their efforts will have the most impact.

For example, you can create a rule set that alerts a salesperson who is particularly skilled at nurturing early-stage prospects when such prospects visit your website. Similarly, you can notify a salesperson who excels at closing deals when near-closing stage prospects are on your website, allowing them to secure the deal.

By utilizing these automations and focusing on the right prospects, you can improve the overall performance of your sales team, resulting in higher revenue and increased commission for your team members.

In summary, using company intent data and sales alerts can significantly enhance your sales and marketing efforts by providing valuable real-time information about prospects' behavior and interests. By acting on this information, you can improve lead conversion, prioritize your sales pipeline, and ultimately drive better results for your organization.

Interactive Content and Chatbots for Conversions and Lead Generation

5.1 The Rise of Interactive Content

In recent years, interactive content has emerged as a powerful tool for marketers seeking to engage, educate, and convert their target audience. The growing popularity of interactive content can be attributed to its unique ability to create two-way conversations between brands and their prospects, offering value for both parties and ultimately driving better results.

Interactive content is dynamic and engaging, demanding active participation from users, whether it's through quizzes, assessments, calculators, or other interactive elements. This type of content not only captures the attention of users but also encourages them to share information about themselves, their needs, and their preferences.

One of the reasons interactive content is so effective is that it's like "stuffing a sales development rep into a piece of content." It enables marketers to educate their audience while simultaneously learning about their prospects. By offering valuable, personalized information to users, marketers can collect detailed profile information about their audience's pain points, challenges, goals, and thought processes.

This data can be used to:

- Lead score: Identify which prospects are most likely to convert based on their engagement with interactive content.

- Define personas: Group your audience into segments based on their characteristics, preferences, and behaviors.

- Qualify prospects: Determine which leads are worth pursuing based on the information they've shared through interactive content.

- Guide the buyer's journey: Use the insights gained from interactive content to create a tailored path for your audience, addressing their unique needs and challenges.

- Create targeted follow-up content: Develop additional content that addresses and ideally helps solve the specific problems or issues your audience faces.

Interactive content allows you to ask and answer questions for your audience in your stead, making it an essential tool for modern marketers looking to drive better results.

The Future of Interactive Content

As consumers continue to demand personalized experiences and marketers look for new ways to engage their audience, the importance of interactive content is only set to grow. By embracing this innovative approach to content marketing, businesses can stay ahead of the curve and deliver value to their audience in a way that drives better outcomes.

To capitalize on the rise of interactive content, marketers should:

- Experiment with different formats: Explore various types of interactive content, such as quizzes, assessments, calculators, and interactive infographics, to find the formats that resonate best with your audience.

- Integrate with existing strategies: Incorporate interactive content into your existing content marketing, lead generation, and nurturing efforts to enhance their effectiveness.

- Optimize for user experience: Ensure that your interactive content is easy to use and visually appealing, creating a seamless experience for users.

- Measure and analyze performance: Track the performance of your interactive content to identify what works, what doesn't, and how you can optimize your efforts for better results.

- Continuously innovate: Stay ahead of the curve by exploring new trends, technologies, and strategies related to interactive content.

The rise of interactive content presents significant opportunities for marketers looking to engage their audience, gather valuable insights, and drive better results. By embracing this approach, businesses can create personalized experiences that resonate with their audience and ultimately lead to more conversions and loyal customers.

5.2 Types of Interactive Content for Lead Generation

Interactive content plays a crucial role in lead generation, as it allows marketers to engage, educate, and capture information about their target audience. By offering personalized, engaging experiences, interactive content can help businesses capture high-quality leads and drive better results. In this chapter, we will explore various types of interactive content that can be used for lead generation purposes.

Quizzes and assessments: Quizzes and assessments are excellent tools for engaging users while gathering insights into their preferences, knowledge, and needs. By asking a series of targeted questions, businesses can collect valuable information that can be used to qualify leads and tailor marketing efforts. For example, a marketing agency might create a quiz to help prospects identify their most significant marketing challenges, using the results to offer tailored solutions and capture leads.

Interactive calculators: Calculators are a useful way to help users understand complex concepts, estimate costs, or evaluate potential benefits. By offering a personalized, interactive experience, businesses can demonstrate value while collecting information about users' needs and preferences. For example, a solar energy company might create a calculator that estimates potential savings based on users' energy consumption and location, capturing leads interested in their services.

Interactive eBooks and whitepapers: Transforming traditional eBooks and whitepapers into interactive experiences can increase engagement and lead capture. By adding elements such as interactive charts, clickable images, and quizzes, businesses can make their content more engaging and collect valuable information about their audience. For example, a software company might create an interactive whitepaper that offers personalized insights based on users' responses to embedded questions.

Interactive infographics: Infographics are an effective way to present complex information in an engaging, visually appealing format. By incorporating interactive elements, businesses can make their infographics even more captivating and collect valuable information about users' interests and preferences. For example, a financial services firm might create an interactive infographic that allows users to explore different investment strategies based on their risk tolerance and goals.

Chatbots and conversational marketing: Chatbots and conversational marketing tools can be used to create personalized, interactive experiences that guide users through a series of questions or prompts. These tools can help businesses capture leads, qualify prospects, and collect valuable information about their audience's needs and preferences. For example, a real estate agency might use a chatbot to guide users through the process of finding their ideal property, collecting information about their preferences and capturing leads.

Interactive videos: Videos are an engaging way to share information, and adding interactive elements can make them even more effective for lead generation. Interactive videos can include clickable hotspots, embedded quizzes, or branching scenarios that allow users to explore content based on their interests. For example, a software company might create an interactive product demo that allows users to explore features based on their specific use case.

By leveraging these different types of interactive content, businesses can create engaging, personalized experiences that capture high-quality leads and drive better results. By experimenting with various formats and incorporating interactive content into their lead generation strategies, marketers can engage their audience, collect valuable insights, and ultimately, boost their conversion rates.

During the past years conversational marketing has become more popular.

Conversational marketing is a powerful way to breathe life into your content and continue the user journey beyond static content. By engaging users in interactive, personalized conversations, conversational marketing helps businesses create more meaningful connections with their audience, driving higher engagement and conversion rates.

Unlike traditional marketing methods that rely on one-way communication, conversational marketing facilitates two-way interactions between businesses and their target audience. This approach allows businesses to gather valuable insights into their audience's preferences, needs, and challenges, while also providing personalized, real-time assistance and guidance.

Here are some ways conversational marketing can complement your existing content and take it to the next level:

- Extend the user journey: Conversational marketing tools, such as chatbots, can pick up where static content leaves off, guiding users through the next steps in their journey. For example, after reading a blog post about best practices for email marketing, a chatbot might engage the reader in a conversation about their specific email marketing challenges and offer tailored recommendations.

- Enhance content consumption: Conversational marketing can help users navigate your content more effectively by providing personalized recommendations based on their interests and needs. Instead of having users sift through a vast library of content, a chatbot can guide them to the most relevant resources, saving time and improving the overall user experience.

- Boost engagement and conversions: By offering personalized, real-time assistance, conversational marketing can help users overcome objections, answer questions, and address concerns, ultimately driving higher engagement and conversion rates. For example, if a user is browsing a product page but hesitates to make a purchase, a chatbot can step in to offer additional information, answer questions, and provide personalized incentives to help close the sale.

- Foster long-term relationships: Conversational marketing can help businesses build stronger, more meaningful relationships with their audience by offering ongoing support, assistance, and personalized content. By maintaining an open line of communication and continually engaging users with relevant, valuable information, businesses can foster long-term customer loyalty and drive repeat business.

By leveraging conversational marketing techniques, businesses can create more engaging, personalized experiences that resonate with their audience, driving higher engagement, conversion rates, and long-term customer loyalty.

5.3 Implementing Chatbots for Improved Customer Engagement

Chatbots have become an increasingly popular tool for businesses looking to improve customer engagement and provide personalized experiences for users across various stages of the buying journey. However, it's crucial to approach chatbot implementation with a well-thought-out strategy, ensuring that the chatbot delivers value to users and complements your existing content and marketing efforts.

One key aspect of successful chatbot implementation is leveraging powerful analytics to monitor performance and optimize the chatbot experience. Without proper analytics, businesses risk losing potential customers due to poorly designed chatbot interactions. For example, a locksmith company once implemented a chatbot that asked users an open-ended question about the type of locking mechanism they had on their doors. This question was not only difficult for users to answer, but it also failed to provide value, resulting in a staggering 90% drop-off rate. Fortunately, platforms like Leadoo provide robust analytics capabilities, which can identify and alert businesses of such issues, allowing them to address and optimize their chatbot experiences.

Here are some essential factors to consider when implementing chatbots for improved customer engagement:

- Personalization: Customize your chatbot to provide tailored experiences for users at different stages of the buying journey. This ensures that each interaction is relevant and valuable, leading to higher engagement rates and more satisfied customers.

- Context-awareness: Ensure that your chatbot can understand the context of user interactions, enabling it to provide more accurate and helpful responses. This may involve integrating the chatbot with your CRM or other data sources to access relevant customer information and history.

- User-friendly design: Design your chatbot to be visually appealing, easy to use, and intuitive. Avoid complex or confusing interactions that may frustrate users and lead to drop-offs.

- Continuous optimization: Monitor your chatbot's performance using analytics and make necessary adjustments based on user feedback and drop-off rates. This iterative approach will ensure that your chatbot remains effective and engaging over time.

- Integration with existing marketing efforts: Ensure that your chatbot complements your existing content and marketing strategies, providing a seamless experience for users across all touchpoints.

Chatbots and conversational marketing offer a wide range of possibilities for generating leads, and their versatility allows businesses to tailor their approach to specific audiences and objectives. By combining the power of interactive experiences with personalized guidance, businesses can create a more engaging and effective lead generation process.

In addition to the previous examples discussed, there are numerous other ways chatbots can be used to generate leads and enhance customer engagement. By exploring a variety of use cases and strategically implementing chatbots into their marketing efforts, businesses can unlock the full potential of conversational marketing for lead generation.

Here are more lead generation examples using chatbots and conversational marketing:

- Appointment scheduling: Chatbots can be used to simplify the appointment scheduling process by gathering the necessary information, such as the desired service, date, and time, and then offering available appointment slots. This can lead to more bookings and a more efficient scheduling process.

- Webinar sign-ups: Chatbots can encourage users to sign up for webinars or online events by providing information about the event, answering questions, and guiding them through the registration process. This can lead to higher attendance and improved lead generation.

- Content promotion: Chatbots can be used to share and promote valuable content such as whitepapers, case studies, and e-books. By offering content that is relevant to a user's interests or needs, chatbots can generate more leads by encouraging users to provide their contact information in exchange for access to the content.

- Free trial sign-ups: Chatbots can be utilized to guide users through the process of signing up for a free trial of a product or service. By answering questions and providing personalized assistance, chatbots can increase the likelihood of users converting into paying customers.

- Product or service consultations: Chatbots can offer users the opportunity to schedule a consultation or product demo with a sales representative. By gathering user information and gauging their interest in a product or service, chatbots can generate high-quality leads for sales teams to follow up on.

- Interactive quizzes and assessments: Chatbots can engage users with interactive quizzes or assessments that help them identify their needs, preferences, or pain points. Based on their responses, chatbots can offer personalized recommendations and capture user information for future marketing efforts.

- Contests and giveaways: Chatbots can be used to promote contests and giveaways, encouraging users to participate by providing their contact information for a chance to win. This can result in increased lead generation and heightened brand awareness.

By incorporating chatbots and conversational marketing into various lead generation strategies, businesses can create more personalized, engaging experiences that ultimately lead to higher conversion rates and more qualified leads.

5.4 Why Contact Forms Alone Don't Work

In today's fast-paced digital landscape, relying solely on contact forms for lead generation can be an ineffective approach. As potential customers progress through the buyer's journey, they encounter various stages and have unique needs at each step. Contact forms are a passive method of capturing leads, providing little assistance or guidance throughout the process, and often failing to address the diverse requirements of prospects at different stages.

Contact forms can be likened to a passive salesperson standing behind a counter, waiting for customers to approach them. This passive approach does not actively engage potential customers, nor does it offer the personalized support they need to make informed decisions. In contrast, interactive content and chatbots act as proactive salespeople, always available to assist clients with their needs, answer questions, and guide them through the buying process.

One of the key drawbacks of contact forms is their limited capacity for engagement and personalization. Unlike interactive content and chatbots, contact forms don't offer real-time feedback or tailored responses based on user input. This lack of interaction can result in missed opportunities to connect with potential leads, as prospects may leave the website without filling out the form if they can't find the information they're looking for or if they don't feel engaged with the content.

Prospects in different stages of the buyer journey have distinct needs and priorities. A generic contact form fails to cater to these varying requirements, making it difficult for businesses to effectively nurture leads and move them down the sales funnel. With interactive content and chatbots, marketers can provide personalized experiences that adapt to each prospect's stage in the buyer journey, offering targeted support and information to address their unique needs.

Contact forms typically capture only basic information, such as name, email address, and phone number. This limited data collection can make it challenging for businesses to gain valuable insights into their leads' preferences, pain points, and behaviors. Interactive content and chatbots, on the other hand, can gather more in-depth information through engaging interactions, helping businesses better understand their prospects and tailor their marketing efforts accordingly.

Additionally, long contact forms can be frustrating and time-consuming for visitors to fill out. Limiting qualifying questions in a contact form may save time but can also lead to a lack of valuable information for sales teams. Conversational elements, such as chatbots or visualbots, allow visitors to easily provide data in a step-by-step manner, reducing frustration and increasing the likelihood of form completion. This approach not only enhances the user experience but also helps businesses collect more accurate and detailed information about their leads, enabling more effective sales follow-up and nurturing.

5.5 Reasons to Choose Chatbots over Contact Forms

If you ask a child whether they want to eat vegetables, the answer is likely to be negative. However, if you ask them whether they prefer carrots or parsnips on their plate, the little one will probably choose one of them almost inadvertently. You allow the child to make a decision, but you don't give them the option to refuse vegetables.

This situation is somewhat similar to using chatbots: a chatbot offers a wide range of choices but does not allow the website visitor to say no. Don't get us wrong — we're not comparing website visitors to children. However, many of us tend to say no more easily, so gentle guidance in the right direction is often helpful.

The advantage of chatbots over contact forms is that they don't allow website visitors to say no easily. We at Leadoo Marketing Technologies often emphasize that contact forms no longer work. In this article, we delve deeper into why contact forms don't work and why you should consider using Leadoo's tools on your website.

Would you like to read this entire article now or skip directly to the most important points found at the end of the article? Did you notice what we did here? You probably got the idea already: let's jump into the topic!

Here are six reasons why you should consider chatbot solutions instead of contact forms.

1. The chatbot doesn't give the option to say no

As mentioned earlier, this is a significant advantage of chatbot solutions compared to contact forms: when a website visitor arrives on the page, they either fill out the contact form or don't. It's very simple.

However, if the website visitor starts a conversation with the chatbot, the virtual assistant guides them towards conversion almost without them noticing. Often, the chatbot's built-in pathways and response options are tailored so that the visitor isn't even given the opportunity to respond with "no thanks, I'm just browsing."

2. The chatbot informs about what happens next

Living in the moment is wonderful, but it doesn't work in everyday life. Whether it's a high school student's school day, a company's team-building day, or a conversation with a chatbot, we often need to know what happens next. The chatbot can tell you this: you can build the chatbot to tell exactly what the next response will be or how things will progress after the conversation.

3. You can guide the visitor's journey, even if the lead is already collected

With chatbots, you can guide the visitor's journey even if they have already left their contact information and converted into a lead. This shows that, in addition to conversions, you care about customer satisfaction and a positive user experience.

4. Understand the customer better by asking what they want to do next

The chatbot understands and asks questions. The small virtual assistant takes into account the website visitor, for example, by inquiring if they want to subscribe to a newsletter or explore other products. The chatbot is a personal and conversational element of your website, and its responses can be customized according to the customer's choices.

5. The chatbot directs to other pages if needed

If the website visitor is particularly curious, a mere conversation with the chatbot may not suffice. The chatbot comes to the rescue, gently directing the visitor to the right pages based on their responses.

6.   Additional sales are possible with a chatbot
The chatbot allows for upselling: you can easily collect the first conversion and then offer additional services. This way, you capture all immediate upselling opportunities.

5.6 Why should you allow your visitors to directly book meetings into your calendar

Relying on contact requests from your website can slow down the sales process, as each request needs to be followed up and scheduled to a calendar. To address this issue, a Calendar Booking feature can be implemented, allowing visitors to instantly book meetings instead of merely leaving a contact request. This is not only convenient for both parties, but it also saves time and resources.

A common concern for many companies is the risk of unqualified meetings. However, with chatbots and conversational elements, it is possible to prequalify visitors before showing them the calendar. Company identification tools, such as those provided by Leadoo, can also help qualify prospects. For instance, an accounting company focusing on clients with €10 million+ in revenue can use personalization to display the calendar only to identified companies with over €10 million in revenue, while showing a static contact form to others.

A Calendar Integration feature can help transform contact requests into calendar bookings. This feature can be used in various scenarios, including direct sales meetings, customer service, recruitment, and as a conversion point on landing pages.

For direct sales meetings, Calendar Integration enables website visitors to book a suitable time for a meeting while discussing with a chatbot and providing valuable qualifying information. Salespeople can then enter the meeting fully prepared and ready to impress prospects with their knowledge.

In customer service, interactive tools can provide an engaging and personal way for customers to get in touch 24/7 and book a suitable time for a meeting. This enhances the overall customer experience and ensures that your customers receive swift, personalized support.

When it comes to recruitment, Calendar Integration can be a game-changer. Juggling interview times with multiple candidates can be challenging, but with this feature, you can integrate the hiring manager's calendar into a chatbot and handle the entire application process smoothly.

Adding interactive solutions to your landing pages allows you to engage with multiple visitor types and offer Calendar Integration as an additional conversion opportunity. This means you can convert the hottest visitors into high-quality meetings right away.

Calendar Integration is a feature that can be integrated with various marketing tools, including platforms like Leadoo, and it is compatible with both Google Calendar and Outlook/Office365 calendars. Integrating calendars with this feature offers four main advantages:

1. Time-saving: Eliminate the back-and-forth mess of scheduling meetings and save time with synchronized calendars.
2. Increased sales process efficiency: Booking meetings directly to the calendar streamlines the sales process for both the prospect and the sales team.
3. More and higher-quality sales meetings: Allowing prospects to schedule meetings at their convenience leads to increased commitment and a higher likelihood of purchasing.
4. Enhanced customer experience: Providing an easy, interactive way for customers to engage with a bot, book meetings, and receive valuable information improves their overall experience with your business.

5.7 Enhancing the customer experience with pricing calculators

One of the key factors influencing a potential buyer's purchasing decision is the price of a product or service. However, many websites do not have readily available or easily accessible pricing information. This can lead to customers leaving the site due to frustration or lack of clarity. To address this issue, pricing calculators can be implemented to provide customers with a transparent and accurate price estimate.

Pricing calculators offer several benefits for both customers and businesses. For customers, they provide a clear understanding of the cost of a product or service, allowing them to compare options more easily. For businesses, pricing calculators can serve as an effective lead generation tool, as customers are more likely to provide their contact information after engaging with a calculator.

Industries that can provide concrete examples of product or service prices, such as construction, renovation, and cleaning, are particularly well-suited for pricing calculators. However, these tools can be adapted to suit various industries with customizable features.

There are two primary methods for building pricing calculator bots. In the first method, the customer provides their contact information before receiving a price estimate. This enables businesses to follow up personally via phone or email and continue the conversation after providing the estimate. In the second method, the bot offers the customer a price estimate immediately after the conversation and then asks for contact information or suggests booking an appointment. This allows customers to quickly decide whether they want to continue with the purchasing process.

A well-designed pricing calculator should consist of simple questions, clarity, and the use of images. It is best to avoid open text fields, as predefined options keep the process quick and easy. By incorporating visual elements, a pricing calculator can effectively engage customers and capture their attention.

Pricing calculators can be created using various tools in Leadoo, such as VisualBots or InpageBots. VisualBots allow for the creation of visually appealing and interactive pricing calculators, while InpageBots offer a more conversational experience with the option to include illustrative images.

5.8 How can discussions help you increase conversions

As users explore the online landscape, they frequently observe that information is readily available at their fingertips. The process is straightforward: the user seeks information, obtains it fresh and enticing, and if a strong thirst for knowledge emerges, they may need to search for answers to additional questions, invest time in finding these answers, and ultimately discover what they seek.

Quite one-dimensional - and worst of all, the accumulated conversions feel forced.

On the other hand, if you want to leave a question on a website, you often find a form that always asks for the same contact information. In addition, at this point, a huge opportunity for misunderstandings often opens up - in other words, an open response field.

The problem is that at this point, the visitor has already spent a considerable amount of time looking for answers to their questions and now has to navigate through another one-dimensional communication channel.

Wouldn't it be easier if there was a way to start a conversation as soon as the visitor arrives on the site?

Why do conversations work?

First, conversations engage and feel personal. Conversations help elevate the mood for an upcoming web visit experience. They are also a great way to build trust between a business and a potential customer.

Let's put it this way: which would make you feel more confident about a company, an informative and clever chat or filling out a faceless form and then waiting uncertainly for a response?

That's what I thought.

Secondly, potential customers often give up with boring, stagnant forms. Interactive solutions, such as chatbots and other conversion tools, occur much less frequently because the website visitor doesn't have to do all the work themselves and the conversation flows smoothly forward all the time. Chatbots, therefore, help the customer throughout, making the experience high-quality.

Thirdly, conversations offer information that might otherwise go unnoticed or be difficult to capture. Traditional website analytics tools help determine where website visitors come from and where they jump off. Instead, they don't tell why visitors may have become frustrated and not converted; only offering anonymous, bland figures.

Conversations and the analytics gathered from them provide much more accurate insights into your audience, allowing you to offer visitors even better conversation and service.

Will a chatbot help me convert through conversations?
Yes - and no. Chatbots are a great aid, but they are not the key to success. They can ruin a well-started journey just like any poorly designed element on your website, if indeed they are poorly designed: the conversation must be top-notch and genuinely help the customer. Service and natural conversations always come first, followed by conversions.

Too often, chatbots are either built directly from a template (and it shows) or are on the page just for the sake of being there (that shows too). These chatbots don't usually answer the visitor's questions: they just try to collect information that can be added to an endless list of leads worth targeting for marketing (Marketing Qualified Leads or MQL). Someone might, for example, try to reach out and sell something to a visitor even if they are not nearly as far along their purchasing journey.

The customer experience isn't great either if the customer feels like they can't find what they're looking for. On the other hand, it doesn't produce particularly good business results - a pretty bad situation where no one really wins.

5.9 How do you make your chatbot stand out from the crowd and produce results?

Here are three tricks - literally three tricks - to keep in mind when using a chatbot for conversations and, through that, gathering conversions.

Tie the bot to context
If your chatbot is found on your homepage, it will encounter numerous visitors at different stages of their buying journey. You need to consider this when offering assistance through your chatbot: make sure you account for different needs and provide concrete steps forward.

If the bot is placed on a product or service-related page, your website visitors will have different questions in mind compared to homepage visitors. Therefore, a generic chatbot cannot genuinely serve potential customers well enough to convert them.

Offer a wide variety of conversion points
You cannot convert all website visitors into paying customers right away, so try to find other types of conversions valuable to your business. For example, a quick consultation call, event

registration, newsletter subscription, or sending an e-guide are excellent conversion points.

None of these will generate revenue within the first day, but don't worry: you are consistently attracting people who were not ready to buy but were interested enough to trust you with their contact information. And we all know that getting up-to-date and accurate contact information is a rare treat nowadays.

Below is an example of a bot that ensures the conversation remains friendly and brand-aligned while still providing information and opportunities for those interacting with the bot.

Stay consistent with your brand 👄
This should go without saying, but let's say it anyway: all elements of your website should reflect your brand, values, and promises to customers. This should be apparent in tone, visual design, and service level, as well as other brand-related aspects and, for example, chatbots.

Make sure that bots follow a consistent line with the rest of the visitor's website experience. There is a significant difference between a polished, brand-aligned chatbot and a quickly assembled, chatbot service provider's look that doesn't match your brand. Always choose a service provider that allows you to customize the bot according to your brand.

At this point, I might toot our own horn (🎺). For example Leadoo's conversion tools include everything you need to turn your conversations into conversions.

You'll get conversation analytics that reveal the types of discussions your visitors have had with the bot. Additionally, you'll have access to various bot types that engage potential customers in the best possible way. You'll also receive information about the identified companies visiting your site, even if they don't leave their contact information. This, in turn, offers you the opportunity to proactively start a conversation with them and demonstrate the level of your service.

Analyzing Customer Journeys and Website Analytics

6.1 Measuring the Impact of Interactive Content and Chatbots

Traditional website analytics can provide valuable insights, but these metrics might not accurately reflect the impact of interactive content and chatbots on user engagement and lead generation.

Traditional website analytics, such as time spent on a page, can be misleading. A user spending three minutes on a page could indicate that the content is engaging, or it could signal that they are struggling to find the information they need. This is where measuring engagement becomes essential, as it can provide a clearer picture of user behavior and content effectiveness.

When evaluating the performance of interactive content and chatbots, two primary metrics should be considered: trigger to engagement and engagement to lead. These metrics offer insights into the effectiveness of chatbot interactions and the subsequent conversion of users into leads.

- Trigger to Engagement: This metric measures the number of users who interact with the chatbot after it is triggered. A high trigger to engagement rate indicates that the chatbot is effectively capturing the attention of users and initiating interactions.

- Engagement to Lead: This metric tracks the number of users who become leads after engaging with the chatbot. A high engagement to lead rate demonstrates that the chatbot is successfully guiding users through the conversation and converting them into valuable leads.

A good conversational marketing platform should also enable marketers to analyze drop-off rates at each stage of the dialogue, as well as provide visualizations of the dialogue flow. This information allows marketers to identify areas for improvement and optimize the chatbot content to better serve users and generate leads.

By shifting the focus from traditional website analytics to metrics that directly reflect user engagement and lead generation, marketers can better understand the true impact of interactive content and chatbots. With this knowledge in hand, they can optimize their chatbot content and improve their overall marketing strategy.

6.2 Mapping the Customer Journey

The buyer journey has evolved significantly in recent years, becoming more complex and multifaceted than ever before. The last-click attribution model, which assigns conversion credit to the final touchpoint before a purchase, no longer provides an accurate representation of the customer journey. To succeed in today's dynamic marketplace, businesses must understand the full spectrum of touchpoints that lead to conversions and tailor their strategies accordingly.

To effectively map the customer journey, it's essential to focus on measuring and analyzing the entire process, from the first touchpoint to the last. This comprehensive approach will help businesses identify which channels are most effective at planting the seeds for conversions and which ones are responsible for harvesting the results.

Key analytics to consider when mapping the customer journey include:

Time to Lead (Days): This metric measures the average time it takes for a user to convert into a lead. By tracking this data, businesses can gain insights into the speed and efficiency of their marketing efforts.

Touchpoints: Understanding the number of touchpoints a customer encounters before converting is crucial to optimizing the customer journey. This metric can help businesses identify gaps in their marketing strategy and make improvements where needed.

Page Views: Monitoring page views can provide valuable insights into user behavior and preferences. This data can be used to refine content and improve overall user experience, leading to higher conversion rates.

Conversion per Session: This metric measures the number of conversions per user session, offering insights into the effectiveness of each touchpoint in driving conversions.

In addition to these analytics, evaluating lead quality is vital for optimizing the customer journey. Combining website analytics data with CRM data can provide a more in-depth understanding of the customer journey and lead quality. By backtracking closed deals and analyzing the associated website engagement, businesses can identify patterns and trends that contribute to successful conversions.

By focusing on mapping the entire customer journey, businesses can gain a deeper understanding of the factors that drive conversions and optimize their marketing strategies to better serve their target audience. This holistic approach will ultimately result in a more effective and efficient marketing strategy that drives growth and success.

6.3 Mapping the Customer Journey: The Importance of Filtering and Concrete Examples

In addition to the key analytics mentioned earlier, filtering and segmenting data based on specific criteria can provide even more insights into the customer journey. By examining the differences in behavior between various customer segments, businesses can better tailor their marketing strategies and optimize the customer journey for each target audience.

For example, consider a premade house manufacturer that wants to understand the differences between leads who already have a plot of land and those who don't. By filtering the data based on this criterion, the manufacturer can identify patterns and preferences unique to each group, allowing them to create targeted marketing campaigns and improve the overall customer experience.

Another example comes from the logistics industry, where businesses might want to analyze the behavior of customers based on company type, industry, revenue size, or whether they are seeking regular transportation services versus one-time transportation. Filtering the data by these criteria can help identify trends and preferences for each segment, enabling businesses to better address the needs of their clients and optimize their marketing efforts accordingly.

Without the ability to qualify leads and filter analytics based on specific criteria, businesses are essentially taking a blindfolded approach to marketing. This can result in inefficient use of resources and missed opportunities for growth. By segmenting and filtering data, businesses can gain valuable insights into the unique needs and preferences of different customer groups, enabling them to create tailored marketing strategies that drive better results.

Understanding the customer journey is essential for identifying the elements that contribute to conversions and refining marketing tactics to better meet the needs of the target audience. By utilizing essential analytics and segmenting data based on specific factors, businesses can uncover valuable information about the unique requirements and preferences of different customer segments. This empowers them to develop customized marketing strategies that deliver improved results and facilitate business growth.

6.4 Analyzing Website Analytics for Insights

Tracking and interpreting website analytics have grown increasingly vital for businesses. By examining these analytics, marketers can uncover significant insights into visitor behavior, preferences, and engagement, ultimately empowering them to make well-informed decisions and enhance marketing strategies. This chapter will delve into the importance of this practice and its impact on marketing success.

1. Comprehensive Filtering for Precise Insights
One of the essential components of analyzing website analytics is the ability to filter data based on various criteria. Comprehensive filtering allows marketers to segment data based on factors such as demographics, behavior, and

engagement, providing a more accurate picture of visitor interactions on the website.

For example, a logistics company may want to analyze visitor data based on industry, company size, or the type of transportation service they are seeking (regular vs. one-time). By filtering the data in this manner, the company can better understand the needs and preferences of different customer segments, enabling them to tailor their marketing strategies accordingly.

2. CRM Integration for a Holistic View
Integrating website analytics with Customer Relationship Management (CRM) systems enables businesses to connect the dots between their online and offline customer interactions. This connection provides a comprehensive understanding of the entire customer journey, from their initial website visit to the final sale or conversion.

CRM integration allows marketers to track the effectiveness of their marketing campaigns and identify the channels and touchpoints that lead to conversions. Furthermore, the integration can help businesses identify which website elements or marketing strategies have the most significant impact on lead quality and conversion rates.

For example, a pre-made house manufacturer may wish to compare the behavior of leads who already have a plot versus those who do not. By integrating their website analytics with their CRM system, they can segment the data and analyze the differences in behavior between these two groups. This information can then inform their marketing strategies to better target and serve each segment.

3. Custom Fields for Deeper Analysis
The ability to include custom fields in website analytics and CRM integration provides businesses with even more granular insights into visitor behavior and preferences. Custom fields allow marketers to capture and analyze additional data points relevant to their industry or specific business needs.

By incorporating custom fields into their analytics, businesses can gain a deeper understanding of their target audience and identify trends or patterns that may not be evident through standard data points. This information can be used to refine marketing strategies and enhance overall business performance.

As we've explored in this chapter, analyzing website analytics for insights is a critical component of a successful digital marketing strategy. By taking advantage of comprehensive filtering, CRM integration, and custom fields, businesses can access a wealth of information about their target audience, helping them to refine their marketing strategies to better serve their customers' needs. As we continue our journey through this book, we will build upon these concepts to further enhance our understanding of effective marketing strategies and drive business growth.

6.5 Understanding Attribution Models

In the realm of digital marketing, understanding the effectiveness of various marketing channels and tactics is crucial to optimizing return on investment (ROI). Attribution models play a significant role in this process, as they help marketers determine how credit for conversions should be allocated across different touchpoints in the customer journey. This chapter will explore the concept of attribution models, their importance in marketing strategy, and the different types of models available to marketers.

1.   The Importance of Attribution Models
Attribution models help marketers make data-driven decisions by shedding light on the performance of different marketing channels and tactics. By understanding how each touchpoint contributes to conversions, marketers can allocate resources more effectively, improve customer experiences, and optimize their overall marketing strategy. Properly implemented attribution models can lead to:

- Increased ROI
- Better resource allocation
- Enhanced understanding of customer behavior
- More accurate performance measurement
- Informed decision-making

2.   Types of Attribution Models

There are several attribution models available to marketers, each with its unique approach to assigning credit for conversions. Some of the most commonly used models include:

a. Last-Click Attribution Model: This model attributes 100% of the conversion credit to the last touchpoint before the conversion occurs. While easy to implement and understand, it may not fully represent the impact of earlier touchpoints in the customer journey.

b. First-Click Attribution Model: In contrast, the first-click model assigns all conversion credit to the initial touchpoint that brought the customer to the website. This model highlights the importance of brand awareness and customer acquisition but may overlook the role of subsequent touchpoints in nurturing leads and driving conversions.

c. Linear Attribution Model: The linear model distributes conversion credit equally across all touchpoints in the customer journey. This approach acknowledges the contribution of each touchpoint but may not accurately reflect the varying levels of influence each touchpoint has on the conversion.

d. Time-Decay Attribution Model: This model allocates more credit to touchpoints that occur closer to the conversion event, with the assumption that more recent interactions have a greater impact on the customer's decision to convert. This model may be more suitable for businesses with longer sales cycles, where nurturing leads is essential.

e. Position-Based Attribution Model (U-Shaped): The position-based model assigns a higher percentage of credit to the first and last touchpoints, with the remaining credit distributed equally among the other touchpoints. This approach recognizes the importance of both customer acquisition and closing the sale, while still acknowledging the role of intermediate touchpoints.

f. Data-Driven Attribution Model: Utilizing machine learning algorithms, the data-driven model assigns credit to each touchpoint based on its actual influence on the conversion. This model provides the most accurate representation of the customer journey but requires a substantial amount of data and advanced analytical capabilities.

3. Choosing the Right Attribution Model

Selecting the appropriate attribution model depends on a variety of factors, including business goals, marketing objectives, and available resources. Marketers should carefully consider each model's advantages and limitations, and may need to test multiple models to determine which best aligns with their specific needs.

As you can now understand, attribution models are essential tools for understanding the effectiveness of marketing channels and tactics in driving conversions. By choosing the right model for their unique circumstances, marketers can make informed decisions, optimize resource allocation, and ultimately achieve better marketing outcomes.

4.   Challenges and Barriers to Adoption

Despite the significant advantages of using attribution models, many companies still struggle to implement them effectively. Some of the common challenges and barriers to adoption include:

a. Limited Resources: Implementing advanced attribution models often requires substantial resources, including time, budget, and skilled personnel. Smaller businesses or those with limited marketing budgets may find it difficult to allocate the necessary resources to build and maintain a robust attribution system.

b. Data Quality and Availability: Attribution models rely on accurate, comprehensive, and consistent data to produce meaningful insights. Companies with fragmented or incomplete data may face challenges in creating an accurate representation of the customer journey and understanding the true impact of their marketing efforts.

c. Complexity: Some attribution models, particularly data-driven models, can be complex and require advanced analytical capabilities. Companies lacking in-house expertise or access to advanced analytics tools may find it challenging to implement and maintain these models.

d. Resistance to Change: In some cases, organizations may be resistant to adopting new methodologies, particularly if they have long-standing processes and practices in place.

Overcoming this resistance can be a significant barrier to the implementation of attribution models.

5.   Leadoo's Attribution Modeling Tool
Leadoo offers a user-friendly attribution modeling tool that requires no setup, helping to address some of the challenges mentioned above. With Leadoo's solution, businesses can leverage the benefits of attribution modeling without investing significant resources, navigating complex analytical processes, or worrying about data quality.

By using Leadoo's attribution modeling tool, companies can:

•   Easily access and implement various attribution models without extensive setup or advanced analytical skills
•   Gain valuable insights into the performance of their marketing channels and tactics
•   Make data-driven decisions to optimize their marketing strategy and allocate resources more effectively
•   Improve customer experiences and drive conversions

While implementing attribution models can be challenging for some organizations, the benefits of understanding the effectiveness of marketing channels and tactics in driving conversions are undeniable. Leadoo's attribution modeling tool simplifies this process, providing businesses with an accessible, user-friendly solution for optimizing marketing strategies and achieving better outcomes.

6.6 Lead Qualification: Scoring and Prioritizing Leads

In the world of sales and marketing, not all leads are created equal. Some may be ready to convert immediately, while others may require further nurturing before they are prepared to make a purchase. Lead qualification is the process of scoring and prioritizing leads based on their likelihood to convert, ensuring that sales teams can focus their efforts on the most valuable prospects.

1. The Power of Asking Questions and Collecting Answers
One of the most effective ways to understand a lead's needs and preferences is by directly asking them questions and collecting their answers. This approach enables businesses to gather accurate and relevant information about leads, rather than relying on assumptions. Chatbots and conversational marketing tools can play a crucial role in facilitating these interactions by engaging leads in real-time, asking pertinent questions, and gathering valuable data that can inform lead scoring and qualification processes.

2. Integrating Conversational Marketing into Lead Scoring
To effectively incorporate conversational marketing and chatbots into your lead scoring system, consider the following steps:

a. Design Engaging Conversations: Develop targeted and engaging conversation flows for your chatbot that address the key factors influencing lead qualification. Focus on asking relevant questions that help you understand a lead's needs, preferences, and readiness to purchase.

b. Collect and Analyze Data: Use the data collected from chatbot interactions to inform your lead scoring model. Analyze the responses to identify patterns, preferences, and potential pain points, which can help you tailor your marketing and sales efforts more effectively.

c. Adjust Scoring Criteria: Based on the insights gathered from conversational marketing, adjust your lead scoring criteria to account for the responses provided by leads during chatbot interactions. This will help you prioritize leads more accurately and effectively.

3. Benefits of Integrating Conversational Marketing into Lead Scoring

By incorporating conversational marketing and chatbots into your lead qualification process, you can:

a. Gain Deeper Insights: Obtain more accurate and in-depth information about leads, enabling you to better understand their needs, preferences, and readiness to purchase.

b. Improve Sales Efficiency: Equip your sales team with valuable data collected from chatbot interactions, allowing them to prioritize and engage leads more effectively, leading to higher conversion rates.

c. Enhance Customer Experience: Create personalized and engaging interactions with leads through chatbots, fostering a stronger connection and increasing the likelihood of conversion.

d. Strengthen Sales and Marketing Alignment: Improve collaboration between sales and marketing teams by leveraging chatbot data to inform lead scoring and qualification processes, ensuring a more focused and coordinated approach to converting leads.

By emphasizing the importance of asking questions and utilizing chatbots in your lead qualification process, you can gather more accurate information, better prioritize leads, and ultimately improve your overall sales and marketing efforts.

Conclusions

7.1 Key takeaways

As we come to the end of this journey exploring the Leadoo philosophy, it is essential to revisit and consolidate the key takeaways that can help you revolutionize your approach to lead generation, sales, and customer experience. Let's recap the most important lessons and insights that we've covered throughout this book:

1. Personalize the Customer Experience: Remember that providing a hyper-personalized experience to your customers is crucial in fostering loyalty and driving engagement. Tailor your messaging, content, and interactions to each customer's unique needs and preferences.

2. Create Value and Gather Information: Focus on helping clients validate their needs while simultaneously gathering valuable information that can aid your sales team. This dual approach will enable you to better understand and serve your customers, ultimately resulting in more successful sales efforts.

3. Keep Your Sales Team Informed: Equip your sales team with up-to-date information about your customers so they can engage with prospects more effectively and close deals faster. Maintaining open communication channels and sharing insights with your sales team is vital for their success.

4. Understand Why and How: Analyze the entire customer journey to gain a comprehensive understanding of why and how clients convert. Use this data to optimize your marketing and sales efforts, leading to increased conversion rates and a stronger bottom line.

5. Embrace Conversational Marketing: Utilize chatbots and conversational marketing to ask questions, collect answers, and interact with prospects in a more personal and engaging manner. This approach will help you better qualify leads and prioritize your sales efforts.

6. Leverage Company Intent Data: Use company intent data to drive conversion and inform your sales team about prospects who visit your website. This information can be particularly valuable for re-engaging lost or frozen deals, as well as for alerting your sales team about pipeline prospects who are actively browsing your site.

7. Implement Attribution Models: Make data-driven decisions by using attribution models to better understand the effectiveness of your marketing efforts. This approach can help you allocate resources more efficiently and improve your overall marketing strategy.

8. Prioritize Lead Qualification: Develop a lead scoring system to prioritize leads and focus your sales team's efforts on the most promising prospects. By assigning scores to leads based on their interactions and information gathered, you can

ensure that your sales team is working on the highest potential opportunities.

By implementing these key takeaways from the Leadoo philosophy, you can transform your lead generation and sales processes, resulting in a more efficient, effective, and customer-centric organization. Keep these lessons in mind as you continue to refine and optimize your marketing and sales strategies, and watch your business thrive in the competitive landscape.

7.2 The Future of Conversion and Lead Generation

As we wrap up our exploration of the Leadoo philosophy, it's essential to look ahead at the future of conversion and lead generation. The digital landscape is constantly evolving, and businesses need to be adaptable and forward-thinking to maintain a competitive edge. Leadoo, as a forerunner in its field, is committed to staying at the forefront of these developments, driven by a passion for helping clients transform their websites into their best-performing sales channels. In this final chapter, we will discuss some emerging trends and technologies that will shape the future of conversion and lead generation, and how Leadoo is poised to embrace and champion these advancements.

1. Artificial Intelligence and Machine Learning: AI and machine learning are becoming increasingly sophisticated and will continue to play a significant role in lead generation and conversion. By automating tasks, analyzing data, and predicting customer behavior, these technologies can help businesses optimize their marketing and sales efforts, enabling them to target the right prospects with highly personalized content and interactions.

2. Omnichannel Marketing: As customers interact with brands across multiple channels and touchpoints, it's crucial for businesses to adopt an omnichannel approach to marketing. This means providing a seamless and consistent experience for customers, regardless of the channel or device they use. By integrating all marketing channels and touchpoints, businesses can better understand the customer journey and tailor their efforts accordingly.

3. Enhanced Customer Data Platforms (CDPs): The importance of collecting, analyzing, and utilizing customer data cannot be overstated. As CDPs become more advanced, businesses will be able to gather more comprehensive and accurate customer data, leading to better-targeted marketing campaigns and more efficient sales processes.

4. Conversational Marketing and Chatbots: Conversational marketing and chatbots will continue to gain traction, allowing businesses to engage with customers in a more personal, dynamic, and interactive manner. This approach can help businesses collect valuable information, qualify leads more

effectively, and provide a more engaging and satisfying customer experience.

5.   Hyper-Personalization: With the increasing availability of customer data, businesses will be able to take personalization to new heights. Hyper-personalization involves using advanced data analytics and AI to tailor marketing and sales efforts to individual customers' needs, preferences, and behaviors. This level of personalization can lead to more effective campaigns, higher conversion rates, and increased customer satisfaction.

6.   Voice Search and Voice Assistants: As voice search and voice assistants become more prevalent, businesses will need to adapt their marketing strategies to cater to this new way of interacting with customers. This may involve optimizing content for voice search, developing voice-activated chatbots, and exploring new ways to engage with customers through voice technology.

7.   Privacy and Data Security: As data privacy concerns continue to grow, businesses will need to prioritize data security and transparency to maintain customer trust. This may involve adopting new data protection measures, being more transparent about data collection and usage practices, and ensuring compliance with data privacy regulations.

Leadoo's dedication to innovation and staying ahead of industry trends ensures that its clients can rely on the company to provide cutting-edge solutions for lead generation and conversion. By investing in research and development, Leadoo strives to create new features and tools that will continue to revolutionize the way businesses interact with their customers and drive sales.

At the heart of Leadoo's success is a deep-rooted passion for helping clients succeed in their marketing and sales efforts. By continuously improving its platform, Leadoo empowers businesses to achieve exceptional results, turning their websites into powerful sales channels that drive growth and customer satisfaction.

By keeping an eye on these emerging trends and technologies, businesses can stay ahead of the curve and position themselves for success in the ever-changing world of conversion and lead generation. As a partner in this journey, Leadoo will continue to innovate, adapt to new technologies, and always prioritize the customer experience to ensure continued growth and success for both the company and its clients.

Thank you for reading

As we reach the end of this book, I would like to extend my heartfelt thanks to each and every one of you for taking the time to read and engage with its content. It is my hope that you have enjoyed this journey and found valuable, practical advice that you can apply to your own business endeavors.

Your feedback and comments are incredibly important to me, as they help shape the future direction of our discussions and ensure that we continue to provide valuable insights and guidance. I promise to personally respond to any messages you send, whether through LinkedIn or email, as I truly value your thoughts and opinions.

Once again, thank you for your time and interest in this book. I look forward to hearing your thoughts and continuing our conversation on the ever-evolving landscape of conversion and lead generation.

Wishing you great success in all your future endeavors!

Mikael da Costa